Theodore Roethke

THE LOST SON
and
OTHER POEMS

BY THEODORE ROETHKE

The Lost Son and Other Poems
Open House

THE LOST SON

and

OTHER POEMS

by

THEODORE ROETHKE

Garden City, New York

DOUBLEDAY & COMPANY, INC.

1948

Some of these poems have appeared in:

The American Mercury, The American Scholar, The Commonweal, Harper's Bazaar, Harper's Magazine, The New Republic, The New Yorker, Partisan Review, Poetry: A Magazine of Verse, Mademoiselle, The Saturday Review of Literature, The Sewanee Review, The Virginia Quarterly Review.

CONTENTS

CONTENTS

I

II

III

IV

I

Cuttings

Sticks-in-a-drowse droop over sugary loam,
Their intricate stem-fur dries;
But still the delicate slips keep coaxing up water;
The small cells bulge;

One nub of growth
Nudges a sand-crumb loose,
Pokes through a musty sheath
Its pale tendrilous horn.

[11]

Cutting
(LATER)

This urge, wrestle, resurrection of dry sticks,
Cut stems struggling to put down feet,
What saint strained so much,
Rose on such lopped limbs to a new life?

I can hear, underground, that sucking and sobbing,
In my veins, in my bones I feel it,—
The small waters seeping upward,
The tight grains parting at last.
When sprouts break out,
Slippery as fish,
I quail, lean to beginnings, sheath-wet.

Root Cellar

Nothing would sleep in that cellar, dank as a ditch,
Bulbs broke out of boxes hunting for chinks in the dark,
Shoots dangled and drooped,
Lolling obscenely from mildewed crates,
Hung down long yellow evil necks, like tropical snakes.
And what a congress of stinks!—
Roots ripe as old bait,
Pulpy stems, rank, silo-rich,
Leaf-mould, manure, lime, piled against slippery planks.
Nothing would give up life:
Even the dirt kept breathing a small breath.

Forcing House

Vines tougher than wrists
And rubbery shoots,
Scums, mildews, smuts along stems,
Great cannas or delicate cyclamen tips,—
All pulse with the knocking pipes
That drip and sweat,
Sweat and drip,
Swelling the roots with steam and stench,
Shooting up lime and dung and ground bones,—
Fifty summers in motions at once,
As the live heat billows from pipes and pots.

Weed Puller

Under the concrete benches,
Hacking at black hairy roots,—
Those lewd monkey-tails hanging from drainholes,—
Digging into the soft rubble underneath,
Webs and weeds,
Grubs and snails and sharp sticks,
Or yanking tough fern-shapes,
Coiled green and thick, like dripping smilax,
Tugging all day at preverse life:
The indignity of it!—
With everything blooming above me,
Lilies, pale-pink cyclamen, roses,
Whole fields lovely and inviolate,—
Me down in that fetor of weeds,
Crawling on all fours,
Alive, in a slippery grave.

Orchids

They lean over the path,
Adder-mouthed,
Swaying close to the face,
Coming out, soft and deceptive,
Limp and damp, delicate as a young bird's tongue;
Their fluttery fledgeling lips
Move slowly,
Drawing in the warm air.

And at night,
The faint moon falling through whitewashed glass,
The heat going down
So their musky smell comes even stronger,
Drifting down from their mossy cradles:
So many devouring infants!
Soft luminescent fingers,
Lips neither dead nor alive,
Loose ghostly mouths
Breathing.

Moss-Gathering

To loosen with all ten fingers held wide and limber
And lift up a patch, dark-green, the kind for lining cemetery
  baskets,
Thick and cushiony, like an old-fashioned door-mat,
The crumbling small hollow sticks on the underside mixed
  with roots,
And wintergreen berries and leaves still stuck to the top,—
That was moss-gathering.
But something always went out of me when I dug loose those
  carpets
Of green, or plunged to my elbows in the spongy yellowish
  moss of the marshes:
And afterwards I always felt mean, jogging back over
  the logging road,
As if I had broken the natural order of things in that swamp-
  land;
Disturbed some rhythm, old and of vast importance,
By pulling off flesh from the living planet;
As if I had committed, against the whole scheme of life,
  a desecration.

Big Wind

Where were the greenhouses going,
Lunging into the lashing
Wind driving water
So far down the river
All the faucets stopped?—
So we drained the manure-machine
For the steam plant,
Pumping the stale mixture
Into the rusty boilers,
Watching the pressure gauge
Waver over to red,
As the seams hissed
And the live steam
Drove to the far
End of the rose-house,
Where the worst wind was,
Creaking the cypress window-frames,
Cracking so much thin glass
We stayed all night,
Stuffing the holes with burlap;
But she rode it out,
That old rose-house,
She hove into the teeth of it,
The core and pith of that ugly storm,
Ploughing with her stiff prow,
Bucking into the wind-waves
That broke over the whole of her,

[18]

Flailing her sides with spray,
Flinging long strings of wet across the roof-top,
Finally veering, wearing themselves out, merely
Whistling thinly under the wind-vents;
She sailed into the calm morning,
Carrying her full cargo of roses.

Old Florist

That hump of a man bunching chrysanthemums
Or pinching-back asters, or planting azaleas,
Tamping and stamping dirt into pots,—
How he could flick and pick
Rotten leaves or yellowy petals,
Or scoop out a weed close to flourishing roots,
Or make the dust buzz with a light spray,
Or drown a bug in one spit of tobacco juice,
Or fan life into wilted sweet-peas with his hat,
Or stand all night watering roses, his feet blue in rubber boots.

Transplanting

Watching hands transplanting,
Turning and tamping,
Lifting the young plants with two fingers,
Sifting in a palm-full of fresh loam,—
One swift movement,—
Then plumping in the bunched roots,
A single twist of the thumbs, a tamping and turning,
All in one,
Quick on the wooden bench,
A shaking down, while the stem stays straight,
Once, twice, and a faint third thump,—
Into the flat-box it goes,
Ready for the long days under the sloped glass:

The sun warming the fine loam,
The young horns winding and unwinding,
Creaking their thin spines,
The underleaves, the smallest buds
Breaking into nakedness,
The blossoms extending
Out into the sweet air,
The whole flower extending outward,
Stretching and reaching.

Child on Top of a Greenhouse

The wind billowing out the seat of my britches,
My feet crackling splinters of glass and dried putty,
The half-grown chrysanthemums staring up like accusers,
Up through the streaked glass, flashing with sunlight,
A few white clouds all rushing eastward,
A line of elms plunging and tossing like horses,
And everyone, everyone pointing up and shouting!

Flower-Dump

Cannas shiny as a slag,
Slug-soft stems,
Whole beds of bloom pitched on a pile,
Carnations, verbenas, cosmos,
Moulds, weeds, dead leaves,
Turned-over roots
With bleached veins
Twined like fine hair,
Each clump in the shape of a pot;
Everything limp
But one tulip on top,
One swaggering head
Over the dying, the newly dead.

Carnations

Pale blossoms, each balanced on a single jointed stem,
The leaves curled back in elaborate Corinthian scrolls;
And the air cool, as if drifting down from wet hemlocks,
Or rising out of ferns not far from water,
A crisp hyacinthine coolness,
Like that clear autumnal weather of eternity,
The windless perpetual morning above a September cloud.

II

My Papa's Waltz

The whiskey on your breath
Could make a small boy dizzy;
But I hung on like death:
Such waltzing was not easy.

We romped until the pans
Slid from the kitchen shelf;
My mother's countenance
Could not unfrown itself.

The hand that held my wrist
Was battered on one knuckle;
At every step you missed
My right ear scraped a buckle.

You beat time on my head
With a palm caked hard by dirt,
Then waltzed me off to bed
Still clinging to your shirt.

Pickle Belt

The fruit rolled by all day.
They prayed the cogs would creep;
They thought about Saturday pay,
And Sunday sleep.

Whatever he smelled was good:
The fruit and flesh smells mixed.
There beside him she stood,—
And he, perplexed;

He, in his shrunken britches,
Eyes rimmed with pickle dust,
Prickling with all the itches
Of sixteen-year-old lust.

Dolor

I have known the inexorable sadness of pencils,
Neat in their boxes, dolor of pad and paper-weight,
All the misery of manila folders and mucilage,
Desolation in immaculate public places,
Lonely reception room, lavatory, switchboard,
The unalterable pathos of basin and pitcher,
Ritual of multigraph, paper-clip, comma,
Endless duplication of lives and objects.
And I have seen dust from the walls of institutions,
Finer than flour, alive, more dangerous than silica,
Sift, almost invisible, through long afternoons of tedium,
Dropping a fine film on nails and delicate eyebrows,
Glazing the pale hair, the duplicate gray standard faces.

Double Feature

With Buck still tied to the log, on comes the light.
Lovers disengage, move sheepishly toward the aisle
With mothers, sleep-heavy children, stale perfume,
  past the manager's smile
Out through the velvety chains to the cool air of night.

I dawdle with groups near the rickety pop-corn stand;
Dally at shop windows, still reluctant to go;
I teeter, heels hooked on the curb, scrape a toe;
Or send off a car with vague lifts of a hand.

A wave of Time hangs motionless on this particular shore.
I notice a tree, arsenical grey in the light, or the slow
Wheel of the stars, the Great Bear glittering colder than snow,
And remember there was something else I was hoping for.

The Return

I circled on leather paws
In the darkening corridor,
Crouched closer to the floor,
Then bristled like a dog.

As I turned for a backward look,
The muscles in one thigh
Sagged like a frightened lip.

A cold key let me in
That self-infected lair;
And I lay down with my life,
With the rags and rotting clothes,
With a stump of scraggy fang
Bared for a hunter's boot.

Last Words

Solace of kisses and cookies and cabbage,
That fine fuming stink of particular kettles,
Muttony tears falling on figured linoleum,
Frigidaires snoring the sleep of plenty,
The psyche writhing and squirming in heavy woolen,—
O worm of duty! O spiral knowledge!

Kiss me, kiss me quick, mistress of lost wisdom,
Come out of a cloud, angel with several faces,
Bring me my hat, my umbrella and rubbers,
Enshroud me with Light! O Whirling! O Terrible Love!

Judge Not

Faces graying faster than loam-crumbs on a harrow;
Children, their bellies swollen like blown-up paper bags,
Their eyes, rich as plums, staring from newsprint,—
These images haunted me noon and midnight.
I imagined the unborn, starving in wombs, curling;
I asked: May the blessings of life, O Lord, descend
   on the living.

Yet when I heard the drunkards howling,
Smelled the carrion at entrances,
Saw women, their eyelids like little rags,
I said: On all these, Death, with gentleness, come down.

III

Night Crow

When I saw that clumsy crow
Flap from a wasted tree,
A shape in the mind rose up:
Over the gulfs of dream
Flew a tremendous bird
Further and further away
Into a moonless black,
Deep in the brain, far back.

River Incident

A shell arched under my toes,
Stirred up a whirl of silt
That riffled around my knees.
Whatever I owed to time
Slowed in my human form;
Sea water stood in my veins,
The elements I kept warm
Crumbled and flowed away,
And I knew I had been there before,
In that cold, granitic slime,
In the dark, in the rolling water.

The Minimal

I study the lives on a leaf; the little
Sleepers, numb nudgers in cold dimensions,
Beetles in caves, newts, stone-deaf fishes,
Lice tethered to long limp subterranean weeds,
Squirmers in bogs,
And bacterial creepers
Wriggling through wounds
Like elvers in ponds,
Their wan mouths kissing the warm sutures,
Cleaning and caressing,
Creeping and healing.

The Cycle

Dark water, underground,
Beneath the rock and clay,
Beneath the roots of trees,
Moved into common day,
Rose from a mossy mound
In mist that sun could seize.

The fine rain coiled in a cloud
Turned by revolving air
Far from that colder source
Where elements cohere
Dense in the central stone.
The air grew loose and loud.

Then, with diminished force,
The full rain fell straight down,
Tunnelled with lapsing sound
Under even the rock-shut ground
Under a river's source,
Under primeval stone.

The Waking

I strolled across
An open field;
The sun was out;
Heat was happy.

This way! This way!
The wren's throat shimmered,
Either to other,
The blossoms sang.

The stones sang,
The little ones did,
And flowers jumped
Like small goats.

A ragged fringe
Of daisies waved;
I wasn't alone
In a grove of apples.

Far in the wood
A nestling sighed;
The dew loosened
Its morning smells.

I came where the river
Ran over stones:
My ears knew
An early joy.

And all the waters
Of all the streams
Sang in my veins
That summer day.

IV

The Lost Son

1. The Flight

At Woodlawn I heard the dead cry:
I was lulled by the slamming of iron,
A slow drip over stones,
Toads brooding wells.
All the leaves stuck out their tongues;
I shook the softening chalk of my bones,
Saying,
Snail, snail, glister me forward,
Bird, soft-sigh me home,
Worm, be with me.
This is my hard time.

Fished in an old wound,
The soft pond of repose;
Nothing nibbled my line,
Not even the minnows came.

Sat in an empty house
Watching shadows crawl,
Scratching.
There was one fly.

Voice, come out of the silence.
Say something.

Appear in the form of a spider
Or a moth beating the curtain.

Tell me:
Which is the way I take;
Out of what door do I go,
Where and to whom?

Dark hollows said, lee to the wind,
The moon said, back of an eel,
The salt said, look by the sea,
Your tears are not enough praise,
You will find no comfort here,
In the kingdom of bang and blab.

Running lightly over spongy ground,
Past the pasture of flat stones,
The three elms,
The sheep strewn on a field,
Over a rickety bridge
Toward the quick-water, wrinkling and rippling.

Hunting along the river,
Down among the rubbish, the bug-riddled foliage,
By the muddy pond-edge, by the bog-holes,
By the shrunken lake, hunting, in the heat of summer.

The shape of a rat?
It's bigger than that.
It's less than a leg

And more than a nose,
Just under the water
It usually goes.

Is it soft like a mouse?
Can it wrinkle its nose?
Could it come in the house
On the tips of its toes?

Take the skin of a cat
And the back of an eel,
Then roll them in grease,—
That's the way it would feel.

It's sleek as an otter
With wide webby toes
Just under the water
It usually goes.

2. The Pit

Where do the roots go?
    Look down under the leaves.
Who put the moss there?
    These stones have been here too long.
Who stunned the dirt into noise?
    Ask the mole, he knows.
I feel the slime of a wet nest.
    Beware Mother Mildew.
Nibble again, fish nerves.

3. The Gibber

At the wood's mouth,
By the cave's door,
I listened to something
I had heard before.

Dogs of the groin
Barked and howled,
The sun was against me,
The moon would not have me.

The weeds whined,
The snakes cried,
The cows and briars
Said to me: Die.

What a small song. What slow clouds. What dark water.
Hath the raine a father? All the caves are ice. Only the snow's
     here.
I'm cold. I'm cold all over. Rub me in father and mother.
Fear was my father, Father Fear.
His look drained the stones.

> What gliding shape
> Beckoning through halls,
> Stood poised on the stair,
> Fell dreamily down?

> From the mouths of jugs
> Perched on many shelves,
> I saw substance flowing
> That cold morning.

[48]

Like a slither of eels
That watery cheek
As my own tongue kissed
My lips awake.

Is this the storm's heart? The ground is unstilling itself.
My veins are running nowhere. Do the bones cast out their
    fire?
Is the seed leaving the old bed? These buds are live as birds.
Where, where are the tears of the world?
Let the kisses resound, flat like a butcher's palm;
Let the gestures freeze; our doom is already decided.
All the windows are burning! What's left of my life?
I want the old rage, the lash of primordial milk!
Goodbye, goodbye, old stones, the time-order is going,
I have married my hands to perpetual agitation,
I run, I run to the whistle of money.

Money money money
Water water water

How cool the grass is.
Has the bird left?
The stalk still sways.
Has the worm a shadow?
What do the clouds say?

These sweeps of light undo me.
Look, look, the ditch is running white!
I've more veins than a tree!
Kiss me, ashes, I'm falling through a dark swirl.

4. The Return

The way to the boiler was dark,
Dark all the way,
Over slippery cinders
Through the long greenhouse.

The roses kept breathing in the dark.
They had many mouths to breathe with.
My knees made little winds underneath
Where the weeds slept.

There was always a single light
Swinging by the fire-pit,
Where the fireman pulled out roses,
The big roses, the big bloody clinkers.

Once I stayed all night.
The light in the morning came slowly over the white
Snow.
There were many kinds of cool
Air.
Then came steam.

Pipe-knock.

Scurry of warm over small plants.
Ordnung! ordnung!
Papa is coming!

A fine haze moved off the leaves;
Frost melted on far panes;

The rose, the chrysanthemum turned toward the light.
Even the hushed forms, the bent yellowy weeds
Moved in a slow up-sway.

5

It was beginning winter,
An in-between time,
The landscape still partly brown:
The bones of weeds kept swinging in the wind,
Above the blue snow.

It was beginning winter,
The light moved slowly over the frozen field,
Over the dry seed-crowns,
The beautiful surviving bones
Swinging in the wind.

Light traveled over the wide field;
Stayed.
The weeds stopped swinging.
The mind moved, not alone,
Through the clear air, in the silence.

     Was it light?
     Was it light within?
     Was it light within light?
     Stillness becoming alive,
     Yet still?

A lively understandable spirit
Once entertained you.
It will come again.
Be still.
Wait.

The Long Alley

1

A river glides out of the grass. A river or a serpent.
A fish floats belly upward,
Sliding through the white current,
Slowly turning,
Slowly.

The dark flows on itself. A dead mouth sings under an old tree.
The ear hears only in low places.
Remember an old sound.
Remember
Water.

This slag runs slow. What bleeds when metal breaks?
Flesh, you offend this metal. How long need the bones mourn?
Are those horns on top of the hill? Yesterday has a long look.

Loo, loo, said the sulphurous water,
There's no filth on a plateau of cinders.
This smoke's from the glory of God.

Can you name it? I can't name it.
Let's not hurry. The dead don't hurry.
Who else breathes here? What does the grave say?
My gates are all caves.

The fiend's far away. Lord, what do you require?
> The soul resides in the horse barn.
Believe me, there's no one else, kitten-limp sister.
> Kiss the trough, swine-on-Friday.
Come to me, milk-nose. I need a loan of the quick.
> There's no joy in soft bones.
For whom were you made, sweetness I cannot touch?
> Look what the larks do.
Luminous one, shall we meet on the bosom of God?
> Return the gaze of a pond.

3

Stay close. Must I kill something else?
Can feathers eat me? There's no clue in the silt.
This wind gives me scales. Have mercy, gristle:
It's my last waltz with an old itch.

> A waiting ghost warms up the dead
> Until they creak their knees:
> So up and away and what do we do
> But barley-break and squeeze.

> Tricksy comes and tricksy goes
> Bold in fear therefore;
> The hay hops in the horse's mouth,
> The chin jumps to the nose.

Rich me cherries a fondling's kiss,
The summer bumps of ha:
Hand me a feather, I'll fan you warm,
I'm happy with my paws.

Gilliflower ha,
Gilliflower ho,
My love's locked in
The old silo.

She cries to the hen,
She waves to the goose,
But they don't come
To let her loose.

If we detach
The head of a match
What do we do
To the cat's wish?
Do we rout the fish?
Will the goat's mouth
Have the last laugh?

4

That was a close knock. See what the will wants.
This air could flesh a dead stick. Sweet Jesus, make me sweat.
Are the flowers here? The birds are.
Shall I call the flowers?

Come littlest, come tenderest,
Come whispering over the small waters,
Reach me rose, sweet one, still moist in the loam,
Come, come out of the shade, the cool ways,
The long alleys of string and stem;
Bend down, small breathers, creepers and winders;
Lean from the tiers and benches,
Cyclamen dripping and lilies.
What fish-ways you have, littlest flowers,
Swaying over the walks, in the watery air,
Drowsing in soft light, petals pulsing.

Light airs! Light airs! A pierce of angels!
The leaves, the leaves become me!
The tendrils have me!

5

Bricks flake before my face. Master of water, that's trees away.
Reach me a peach, fondling, the hills are there.
Nuts are money: wherefore and what else?
Send down a rush of air, O torrential,
Make the sea flash in the dust.

Call off the dogs, my paws are gone.
This wind brings many fish;
The lakes will be happy:
Give me my hands:
I'll take the fire.

A Field of Light

I

Came to lakes; came to dead water,
Ponds with moss and leaves floating,
Planks sunk in the sand.

A log turned at the touch of a foot;
A long weed floated upward;
An eye tilted.

Small winds made
A chilly noise;
The softest cove
Cried for sound.

Reached for a grape
And the leaves changed;
A stone's shape
Became a clam.

A fine rain fell
On fat leaves;
I was there alone
In a watery drowse.

[57]

2

Angel within me, I asked,
Did I ever curse the sun?
Speak and abide.

Under, under the sheaves,
Under the blackened leaves,
Behind the green viscid trellis,
In the deep grass at the edge of field,
Along the low ground dry only in August,—

Was it dust I was kissing?
A sigh came far.
Alone, I kissed the skin of a stone;
Marrow-soft, danced in the sand.

3

The dirt left my hand, visitor.
I could feel the mare's nose.
A path went walking.
The sun glittered on a small rapids.
Some morning thing came, beating its wings.
The great elm filled with birds.

Listen, love,
The fat lark sang in the field;
I touched the ground, the ground warmed by the kill-
    deer,

The salt laughed and the stones;
The ferns had their ways, and the pulsing lizards,
And the new plants, still awkward in their soil,
The lovely diminutives.
I could watch! I could watch!
I saw the separateness of all things!
My heart lifted up with the great grasses;
The weeds believed me, and the nesting birds.
There were clouds making a rout of shapes crossing
    a windbreak of cedars,
And a bee shaking drops from a rain-soaked honey-
    suckle.
The worms were delighted as wrens.
And I walked, I walked through the light air;
I moved with the morning.

The Shape of the Fire

1

What's this? A dish for flat lips.
Who says? A nameless stranger.
Is he a bird or a tree? Not everyone can tell.

Water recedes to the crying of spiders.
An old scow bumps over black rocks.
A cracked pod calls.

Mother me out of here. What more will the bones
    allow?
Will the sea give the wind suck? A toad folds
    into a stone.
These flowers are all fangs. Comfort me, fury.
Wake me, witch, we'll do the dance of rotten sticks.

Shale loosens. Marl reaches into the field. Small birds pass
    over water.
Spirit, come near. This is only the edge of whiteness.
I can't laugh at a procession of dogs.

In the hour of ripeness the tree is barren.
The she-bear mopes under the hill.
Mother, mother, stir from your cave of sorrow.

[60]

A low mouth laps water. Weeds, weeds, how I love you.
The arbor is cooler. Farewell, farewell, fond worm.
The warm comes without sound.

2

Where's the eye?
The eye's in the sty.
The ear's not here
Beneath the hair.
When I took off my clothes
To find a nose,
There was only one shoe
For the waltz of To,
The pinch of Where.

Time for the flat-headed man. I recognize that listener,
Him with the platitudes and rubbery doughnuts,
Melting at the knees, a varicose horror.
Hello, hello. My nerves knew you, dear boy.
Have you come to unhinge my shadow?
Last night I slept in the pits of a tongue.
The silver fish ran in and out of my special bindings;
I grew tired of the ritual of names and the assistant keeper
   of the molluscs:
Up over a viaduct I came, to the snakes and sticks of another
   winter,
A two-legged dog hunting a new horizon of howls.
The wind sharpened itself on a rock;
A voice sang:

[61]

Pleasure on ground
Has no sound,
Easily maddens
The uneasy man.

Who, careless, slips
In coiling ooze
Is trapped to the lips,
Leaves more than shoes;

Must pull off clothes
To jerk like a frog
On belly and nose
From the sucking bog.

My meat eats me. Who waits at the gate?
Mother of quartz, your words writhe into my ear.
Renew the light, lewd whisper.

3

The wasp waits.
       The edge cannot eat the centre.
The grape glistens.
       The path tells little to the serpent.
An eye comes out of the wave.
       The journey from flesh is longest.
A rose sways least.
       The redeemer comes a dark way.

[62]

Morning-fair, follow me further back
Into that minnowy world of weeds and ditches,
When the water-birds floated high over the white houses,
And the little crabs slipped into silvery craters,
When the sun for me glinted the sides of sand grain
And my intent stretched over the buds at their first trembling.

That air and shine: and the flicker's loud summer call:
The bearded boards in the stream and the all of apples;
The glad hen on the hill; and the trellis humming.
Death was not. I lived in a simple drowse:
Hands and hair moved through a dream of wakening blossoms.
Rain sweetened the cave and the dove still called;
The flowers leaned on themselves, the flowers in hollows;
And love, love sang toward.

5

To have the whole air!—
The light, the full sun
Coming down on the flowerheads,
The tendrils turning slowly,
A slow snail-lifting, liquescent;
To be by the rose
Rising slowly out of its bed,
Still as a child in its first loneliness;
To see cyclamen veins become clearer in early sunlight,
And mist lifting, drifting out of the brown cat-tails;

To stare into the after-light, the glitter left on the lake's sur-
    face
When the sun has fallen behind a wooded island;
To follow the drops sliding from a lifted oar,
Held up, while the rower breathes, and the small boat drifts
    quietly shoreward;
To know that light falls and fills, often without our knowing,
As an opaque vase fills to the brim from a quick pouring,
Fills and trembles at the edge yet does not flow over,
Still holding and feeding the stem of the contained flower.